Mark Water

HUNT&
THORPE

Copyright © 1994 Hunt & Thorpe
Text © 1994 Mark Water
Illustrations © Sue Climpson
Originally published by Hunt & Thorpe
in black and white 1994
Typography by Jim Weaver Design

ISBN 1 85608 243 1

In Australia this book is published by:
Hunt & Thorpe Australia Pty Ltd.
9 Euston Street, Rydalmere NSW 2116

The right of Mark Water and Sue Climpson to be
identified as author and illustrator of this work has been
asserted by them in accordance with the Copyright,
Designs and Patents Act 1988

A CIP catalogue record for this book is available
from the British Library

Manufactured in Singapore

INTRODUCTION

'It's the thought that counts' is generally accepted as true, even when we are not thrilled with the gift. To be in someone's thoughts is itself a privilege and encouragement. We know the truth of this. We have felt the kind word, the thoughtful gesture, the sympathetic silence that tells us we're not alone.

But above all, we know that God is ever mindful of us. He knows each one of us by name. God's knowledge of us is overwhelming, as the psalmist tell us. God knows our problems, our weaknesses. He knows the strength we need.

Throughout the ages, men and women have found the strength of God. Their words encourage us and show us how we may discover the goodness of God each moment of our lives. 'The way from God to a human heart,' wrote S.D. Gordon, 'is through a human heart.'

*A*ll will be well,

and all will be well,

and all manner of things

will be well.

JULIAN OF NORWICH, 1342-1416,
Revelations of Divine Love

*Let us help one another
to bear the burdens of life.*

VOLTAIRE,
1694-1778

Readiness and ability for any work is not given before the work, but only through the work.

ANDREW MURRAY,
1828-1917

The Lord is my shepherd,
I shall ~~not want~~ be in want.

THE BIBLE,
PSALM 23:1

The King of Love my Shepherd is,
Whose goodness faileth never;
I nothing lack, if I am His,
And He is mine for ever.

H.W. BAKER,
1821-1877

Truly it is in the darkness that one finds the light, so when we are in sorrow, then this light is nearest of all to us.

MEISTER ECKHART,
1260-1327

As for me
I believe in nothing
but miracles.

WALT WHITMAN,
1819-1892

Ask, and it shall be given you;
Seek, and ye shall find;
Knock, and it shall be
opened unto you.

THE BIBLE, JESUS CHRIST,
LUKE 11:9 AV

Let your hook be always cast;
in the pool where you least expect
it, there will be a fish.

OVID,
43BC-AD17

Boundless is thy love for me,
Boundless then my trust shall be.

ROBERT BRIDGES,
1844-1930

The real voyage of discovery
consists not in seeking new
landscapes but in having new eyes.

MARCEL PROUST,
1871-1922

Trust the past to God's mercy,
the present to his love, and the
future to his providence.

AUGUSTINE,
354-430

Whatever your hand finds to do, do it with all your might, for in the grave, where you are going, there is neither working nor planning nor knowledge nor wisdom.

THE BIBLE,
ECCLESIASTES 9:10

You are but a poor soldier of Christ if you think you can overcome without fighting.

JOHN CHRYSOSTOM
c345-407

When the day that he must go hence was come, many accompanied him to the Riverside, in which, as he went, he said, Death where is thy sting?...

...*And as he went deeper he said, Grave, where is thy victory? And so he passed over, and the trumpets sounded for him on the other side.*

JOHN BUNYAN, 1628-1688,
Pilgrim's Progress

To him who is able to do immeasurably more than all we ask or imagine, according to his power at work within us, to him glory.

THE BIBLE, THE APOSTLE PAUL,
EPHESIANS 3:20

Life is not a holiday, but an education. And the one eternal lesson for us all is how better we can love.

HENRY DRUMMOND
1851-1897

How ow sweet the name of
Jesus sounds In a believer's ear!
It soothes his sorrows, heals his
wounds, And drives away his fear!

JOHN NEWTON,
1725-1807

Faith is not an effort, a striving, a ceaseless seeking, as so many earnest souls suppose, but rather a letting go, an abandonment, an abiding rest in God.

AUTHOR UNKNOWN

*Prayer is a powerful thing,
for God has bound and tied
himself thereto. None can believe
how powerful prayer is, and what
it is able to effect, but those who
have learned it by experience.*

MARTIN LUTHER,
1483-1546

The braver as he realises his own powerlessness; all the bolder as he sees his own weakness; for all his confidence is in God.

FRANCIS DE SALES,
1567-1622

He is not dead, this friend, not dead, But, in the path we mortals tread, Gone some few, trifling steps ahead...

...*And nearer to the end;*

So that you, too, once past the bend,

Shall meet again, as face to face,

this friend you fancy dead.

ROBERT LOUIS STEVENSON,
1850-1894

Those who live in the Lord never see each other for the last time.

GERMAN PROVERB

*L*eave results to God.

ELIZABETH BARRETT BROWNING,
1806-1861

I always thank God

for you.

THE BIBLE, THE APOSTLE PAUL,
1 CORINTHIANS 1:4

And my God will meet all your needs according to his glorious riches in Christ Jesus.

THE BIBLE, THE APOSTLE PAUL,
PHILIPPIANS 4:19

A man can do only what he can do. But if he does that each day he can sleep at night and do it again the next day.

ALBERT SCHWEITZER,
1875-1965

Let me not beg for the

stilling of my pain, but for the

heart to conquer it.

RABINDRANATH TAGORE
1861-1941

*The Lord gets his best soldiers
out of the highlands of adversity.*

C.H. SPURGEON,
1834-1892

Boundless is Thy love for me,
Boundless too my trust shall be.

ROBERT BRIDGES,
1834-1930

Do not be anxious about anything, but in everything, by prayer and petition, with thanksgiving, present your requests to God.

THE BIBLE, THE APOSTLE PAUL,
PHILIPPIANS 4:6

When you love somebody, you love him as he is.

CHARLES PEGUY,
1873-1914

Love one another in truth and purity, as children, impulsively and uncalculatingly.

EDWARD WILSON'S DIARY,
*member of Scott's last expedition
to the Antarctic.*

Come to me, all you who are weary and burdened, and I will give you rest.

THE BIBLE, JESUS CHRIST,
MATTHEW 11:28

Take my yoke upon you and learn from me, for I am gentle and humble in heart, and you will find rest for your souls.

THE BIBLE, JESUS CHRIST,
MATTHEW 11:29

*Give no place to despondency.
This is a dangerous temptation
of the adversary. Melancholy
contracts and withers the heart.*

MADAME GUYON,
1648-1717

So long as we are loved by others
I would almost say that we are
indispensable.

ROBERT LOUIS STEVENSON,
1850-1894

He [God] gives strength

to the weary and increases

the power of the weak.

THE BIBLE,
ISAIAH 40:29

Those who hope in the Lord

will renew their strength...

*...They will soar on wings like
eagles; they will run and not
grow weary, they will walk
and not be faint.*

THE BIBLE,
ISAIAH 40:31

Do all the good you can, By all the means you can, In all the ways you can, In all the places you can, To all the people you can, As long as ever you can.

JOHN WESLEY,
1703-1791

Tears are sometimes more

eloquent than words.

OVID,
43BC-AD17

He [God] will wipe every tear from their eyes. There will be no more death or mourning or crying or pain, for the old order of things has passed away.

THE BIBLE,
REVELATION 21:4

Call the world if you please
'The Vale of Soul-making.'
Then you will find out the
use of the world.

JOHN KEATS,
1795-1821

Love seeketh not itself to please

Nor for itself hath any care,

But for another gives its ease

And builds a heaven in hell's despair.

WILLIAM BLAKE,
1757-1827

For the love of God is broader

Than the measures of man's mind,

And the heart of the Eternal

Is most wonderfully kind.

F.W. FABER,
1814-1863

Weeping may remain for a night,
but rejoicing comes in the morning.

THE BIBLE,
PSALM 30:5

There is precious instruction

to be got by finding out

where we went wrong.

THOMAS CARLYLE,
1795-1881

Teach me to live, that I may dread
The grave as little as my bed;
Teach me to die, that so I may
Rise glorious at the awful day.

BISHOP THOMAS KEN,
1637-1711

*I'll act with prudence as far as
I'm able; But if success I must
never find, Then come misfortune,
I bid thee welcome, I'll meet thee
with an undaunted mind.*

ROBERT BURNS,
1759-1796

*I*n the world to come
I shall not be asked: 'Why were
you not Moses?' But God will ask
me, 'Why were you not Zusya?'

RABBI ZUSYA, A JEWISH SCHOLAR,
JUST BEFORE HIS DEATH

Then first I knew the delight of being lowly; of saying to myself; 'I am what I am, nothing more.'

GEORGE MACDONALD,
1824-1905

Extreme busyness, whether at school or college, kirk or market, is a symptom of deficient vitality.

R.L. STEVENSON,
1850-1894

Whatsoever thy hand findeth to do, do that with thy might and leave the issues calmly to God.

THOMAS CARLYLE,
1795-1881

We know that in all things God works for the good of those who love him.

THE BIBLE, THE APOSTLE PAUL,
ROMANS 8:28

*True holiness consists in doing
God's will with a smile.*

MOTHER TERESA OF CALCUTTA,
BORN 1910

Lead us, heavenly Father, lead us

O'er the world's tempestuous sea...

...*Guard us, guide us,*

keep us, feed us,

For we have no help but thee...

...Yet possessing

every blessing

If our God our Father be.

J. EDMESTON,
1791-1867

Blessed is the influence of one true, loving soul on another.

GEORGE ELIOT,
1819-1890

*Not what thou art
nor what thou hast been does
God regard with his merciful eyes,
but what thou wouldest be.*

THE CLOUD
OF UNKNOWING

Be not afraid to pray –
to pray is right. Pray, if thou
canst, with hope; but ever pray,
though hope be weak, or sick with
long delay; pray in the darkness,
if there be no light.

HARTLEY COLERIDGE,
1796-1849

I have learned the secret of being content in any and every situation.

THE BIBLE, THE APOSTLE PAUL,
PHILIPPIANS 4:12

What the caterpillar calls
the end of the world,
the master calls a butterfly.

RICHARD BACH

... 'God doth not need Either man's work or his own gifts, who best Bear his mild yoke, they serve him best, his State is Kingly...

...Thousands at his bidding speed
And post o'er land and ocean
without rest: They also serve who
only stand and wait.

JOHN MILTON, 1608-1674,
ON HIS BLINDNESS

*We are always getting ready
to live but never living.*

R.W. EMERSON,
1803-1882

*There are no disappointments
to those whose wills are buried
in the will of God.*

F.W. FABER,
1814-1863

Jesu? the very thought of thee
With sweetness fills my breast;
But sweeter far thy face to see
And in thy presence rest.

12TH CENTURY, TRANSLATED
E. CASWALL, 1858

*Evil, once manfully fronted,
ceases to be evil; there is generous
battle-hope in place of dead,
passive misery.*

THOMAS CARLYLE,
1795-1881

With God

all things are possible.

THE BIBLE, JESUS CHRIST,
MATTHEW 19.26

Dear Lord, of Thee three things I pray: To know Thee more clearly, Love Thee more dearly, Follow Thee more nearly Day by day.

RICHARD OF CHICHESTER,
1197-1253

I am only one. I can't do everything, but that won't stop me from doing the little I can do.

EVERETT HALE,
1822-1909

*It is not great talents
God blesses so much as
great likeness to Jesus.*

MURRAY MCCHEYNE

Are not two sparrows sold for a penny? Yet not one of them will fall to the ground apart from the will of your Father...

THE BIBLE, JESUS CHRIST,
MATTHEW 10:29

...So don't be afraid;

you are worth more than

many sparrows.

THE BIBLE, JESUS CHRIST,
MATTHEW 10:31

I know not what the future hath
Of marvel or surprise;
Assured of this, that life and death
His mercy underlies.

J.G. WHITTIER,
1807-1892

All I have seen teaches me
to trust the Creator for all
I have not seen.

R.W. EMERSON, 1803-1882

The biggest disease today is not leprosy or tuberculosis, but rather the feeling of being unwanted, uncared for, and deserted by everybody.

MOTHER TERESA OF CALCUTTA,
BORN 1910

I no longer call you servants.
...Instead, I have called you
friends, for everything that I have
learned from my Father I have
made known to you.

THE BIBLE, JESUS CHRIST,
JOHN 15:15

*Nothing is really ours
until we share it.*

C.S. LEWIS,
1898-1963

*N*o *Goliath*

is bigger than God.

AUTHOR
UNKNOWN

What is this life

If full of care

We have no time

To stand and stare?

W.H. DAVIES,
1871-1940

My grace is

sufficient for you,

for my power is made perfect

in weakness.

THE BIBLE, THE APOSTLE PAUL,
2 CORINTHIANS 12:9